BABY ANIMALS

Ponies
and foals

Kate Petty

BARRON'S

Mother and baby

A mother pony, or mare, likes to have her baby alone and at night. The foal has grown inside her for about 11 months but now it is born very quickly. The foal's eyes are open and it makes little nickering noises. It tries to stand up almost right away, but the mother washes it all over before she allows it to get to its feet.

The foal's mother gets to know its smell from the beginning.

This Dulmen pony will have her foal soon. ▷

Standing alone

Most foals are on their feet less than an hour after being born. Ponies are animals that live naturally with a group, so they need to be on the move as soon as possible. Once the foal can stand, the mother helps it to find the two teats close to her back legs so that it can drink her milk. The young foal stays close to its mother all the time at first, feeding little and often.

A young foal drinks milk from its mother.

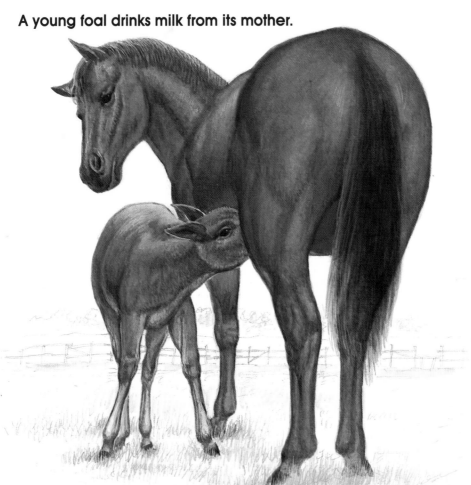

A New Forest pony foal struggles to its feet. ▷

First steps

The new foal takes its first tottering steps as soon as it can stand. Within the next few hours it learns to gallop and play and even to swim if it has to! But it is still a baby that needs to sleep for much of the time. Young foals lie on the grass to rest. As they get older they often rest standing up although they will always need to sleep lying flat on their sides.

A foal takes its first wobbly steps.

This new Shetland pony foal soon walks alongside its mother wherever she goes. ▷

A closer look

A pony can see, hear and smell as soon as it is born. A pony's eyes are twice as large as human eyes and it can see fairly well in the dark. A pony can see almost all around without moving its head. Ponies have a remarkable sense of hearing. They can twist their ears around one at a time to pick up the smallest sound. With their huge nostrils they also have an excellent sense of smell. A mare can pick out her foal in the dark by its smell.

The pony has beautiful, large eyes and big, sensitive nostrils.

With its ears pricked up this little Dales pony foal is listening carefully. ▷

Food and drink

A foal drinks milk from its mother until it is about nine months old but it starts to nibble at grass too, during its first month. Ponies have small stomachs so they need to feed often. If they live in fields they like to graze for many hours in a day, eating flowers, fruits and roots as well as grasses. Domestic ponies need hay in winter and there should always be plenty of water to drink.

Ponies feed happily on hay when grass is scarce.

A tiny Falabella horse grows to only 7.2 hands (30in). ▷

Pony motion

The little pony's long, slim legs look fragile but they are really quite strong. Ponies move their legs in different ways at different speeds. The walking pony puts its feet down one at a time, but when trotting its feet touch the ground two at a time in diagonal pairs. Racing ponies can gallop at about 31 mph and many ponies can jump over obstacles higher than themselves.

Pony trotting

A New Forest pony foal cantering ▷

Ponies at play

Very young foals are playful and inquisitive. From about three months the foals will play together, chasing one another across a field and play-fighting. Male foals (called colts) fight far more than females (called fillies). Surprisingly, adult ponies – even the male stallions – don't seem to mind when the young colts launch playful attacks on them.

A pony foal enjoying a gallop

New Forest pony foals playfully attacking each other ▷

Horsetalk

The mother pony and her foal "talk" with little nickering sounds and each can recognize the other's voice. Ponies snort with curiosity, whicker in greeting and neigh to keep in touch with other ponies. But ponies communicate in other ways too. Their ears and lips are very expressive, so is the way they hold their tail.

Pony expressions

curiosity

worry

anger

disgust

Piebald foals having a nuzzle and a "chat" ▷

A herd of ponies

Wild ponies live in groups, or herds, of six or seven animals or more. A herd might consist of one stallion with two or three mares together with their foals and older offspring. Ponies often have a special friend within the herd. Friends nibble one another's manes and standing head to tail will swat the flies from each other's faces.

Many Camargues still live wild on the marshes in France.

A Dulmen pony foal grooming its friend ▷

Growing up

The mother pony may lose interest in her foal after the first year when she has a new one to take care of. Wild colts usually move away from the herd before they are two years old. At four or five years the pony is fully grown at about 14 hands high (55in) at the shoulder although many breeds are much smaller. By five years old they are able to produce babies of their own.

Many ponies are tiny compared with some breeds of horses.

Shetlands are measured in inches. This foal will grow to 35 inches (90cm) high. ▷

Pony facts

Ponies are the smaller breeds of horses being no bigger than 14.2 hands high (57in). The tiny, dog-sized Falabella is too small to be ridden, although young children can ride on little Shetland ponies which are stronger. Most ponies are good with children as well as being strong and hardworking. Ponies can often live to be 20 – the oldest one on record died at the age of 54!

Newborn

Adult female

Adult male

Index

A
age 22

B
birth 2, 4

C
Camargue 18, 19
cantering 12
colt 14, 20
communicating 16

D
Dales pony 9
Dulmen pony 3, 19

E
ears 8, 9, 16
expressions 16
eyes 8

F
Falabella 11, 22
feeding 10
filly 14
friends 18

G
galloping 6, 12, 14
grazing 10, 11
grooming 18

H
hay 10

J
jumping 12

M
mare 2, 8, 18

N
New Forest pony 5, 13
nostrils 8

P
Piebald foals 17
playing 6, 14, 15
pregnancy 2, 3

R
resting 6

S
senses 2, 8
Shetland pony 7, 21
size 20
stallion 14, 18
standing 4
swimming 6

T
tail 16
trotting 12

W
walking 6, 7, 12

Photographic credits:

Cover and pages 3, 5, 11, 13, 17, 19 and 21: Bruce Coleman Ltd; pages 7 and 9: J. Allan Cash Library; page 15: Ardea

Design	David West Children's Book Design
Illustrations	George Thompson
Picture Research	Cee Weston-Baker

First paperback edition for the United States and Canada published 1993 by Barron's Educational Series, Inc.

First published in the United States 1990 by Gloucester Press.

© Copyright 1989 by Aladdin Books Ltd

All inquiries should be addressed to:
Barron's Educational Series, Inc.
250 Wireless Boulevard
Hauppauge, NY 11788

Library of Congress
Catalog Card No. 90-32381
International Standard
Book No. 0-8120-1487-1 (paperback)

Library of Congress Cataloging-in-Publication Data

Petty, Kate.
    Ponies and foals/ Kate Petty.
    p.cm.—(Baby animals)
    Summary: Describes how ponies and foals are born and grow, how they learn to walk, how they are fed at first, and how they communicate.
    ISBN 0-8120-1487-1 (paperback)
1. Ponies—Juvenile literature. 2. Foals—Juvenile literature. (1. Ponies. 2. Horses. 3. Animals—Infancy.) I. Title. II Series: Petty, Kate. Baby animals.
SF315.P48   1990
636. 1'6—dc20   90-32381
                                 CIP AC

PRINTED IN BELGIUM

3456   987654321